Dear Julie Bryan
With much love
Gladys
x+x+

To all my family and my friends who
joined me on my walking emails
journey

Thank you!

Introduction

In 2020 the corona virus pandemic struck the world. Britain, like most countries, started to worry. Long queues formed at shops and panic buying became the latest craze. The health service was under pressure and the advice was for vulnerable people to self-isolate. To keep myself active and fit, I set myself the challenge to walk non-stop every day, except Sundays, for at least half to three-quarters of an hour.

I decided to find out if any of my friends or family wanted to get involved and so I sent out an invite via email.

What follows are the daily emails I sent plus some of the many wonderful replies I had back from those that joined me on my journey.

12th March

Gladys

My brother, Brian, said he was out in his car this morning and followed a van which had a notice at the rear which read:
No toilet rolls are stored in this vehicle overnight
Xxx

18th March

Gladys

Emails to friends and family sent, asking if they would like to join me for daily exercise, around the house and garden, whilst I choose an outfit from my wardrobe.

Shirley

I'm going to hobble around as long as possible to keep you company. Starting tomorrow. X

19th March

Gladys

Listened to Elvis Presley- 'If I can dream' whilst wearing a diamante bikini.

20th March

Gladys

Wore Madonna's conical bra and costume whilst listening to Rod Stewart

21st March

Gladys

Now for traditional Jazz, with Chris Barber wearing pedal pusher pants, t-shirt and a ponytail.

Wendy

All done with a short intermission. As I was passing a certain room I just had to pop in. Soon got into the swing again with renewed energy. Will go for an outside walk later. Rather cold at the moment. See you Monday so to speak. Wendy x

23rd March

Gladys

A bit frenetic today, wore an orange jumpsuit whilst listening to Saturday night fever.

Jo

Did my 3000 to Co-op. Absolutely NO veg, salad or fruit. Lovely fresh air though - just as well, as it looks as if I'll be living on that from now on!

The Lockdown begins.....

Complete shutdown for at least two months.

Gladys

Hi, everyone, in view of yesterday's news, I am walking to Rachmaninov piano concerto no 2! Surprised? Not when you realise it is the music from my most favourite film Brief Encounter. It was made when Britain had just come through the war. I am wearing skirt jumper a la Celia Johnson with a turban hat and clutch bag. At least it will make you happy that we no longer talk with clipped voices, get our library books from Boots the chemist have an organist play halfway through a film session or wear those fashions! Think I shall watch the dvd this afternoon. Love it
Lots love everyone xxxx

Jacqui

"I wonder, could you help me out of the most appalling domestic lie.." or have I misquoted Miss Johnson? I'm setting off in a few mins to Fleetwood Mac.

25th March

Gladys

The house opposite mine has 2 children, I opened my curtains this morning to see very cheerful decorated windows, lifted the gloom and had a 'shout' with the children and their mum and another neighbour, so good start to the day.

As yesterdays 'walk music costume' was a bit depressing, I am upping my music and clothes today. I shall be setting off as usual round the house and garden at 9.30, listening to Bette Midler and wearing a red basque, suspender belt and

stockings!

For those of you who have been with me from the start, we have been together for a week. So well done and keep moving. Perhaps we should move to the US, Trump says it will be all over there by Easter!!!!

Xxxx

Eileen

How lovely. Let's hope the parents can keep the initiative fresh for the duration. Have been using my garden as a track this morning in the sunshine. I run across the back, along the grass , down the steps, then reverse it. I was quite out of puff after 10 laps

26th March

Gladys

Bit late with the e mail today, just had phone call from my friend in Australia- same as here over there!

Anyway today I thought after looking like a porn star yesterday I would be a bit more delicate and wear jeans and a jumper while walking listening to and (remembering my youth) the one and only Frank Sinatra. Songs for swinging lovers

Keep moving xxx

27th March

Gladys

I shall just be walking to radio 2 today setting off at 9.30. My younger brother Brian was taken into hospital last night with severe breathing difficulties. He has COPD and is in isolation, don't know if it is corona yet. You will have all seen him at my 80th so please love and thoughts for him and Maureen.
Gladysxx

Daphne

Will be joining walks in form of bending exercise cos flat small & would have to walk in front of tv (Chris would not be a happy bunny!! Joining all in sending love to Brian & Maureen. Thoughts with him xx

28th March

Gladys

Hi, everyone, I shall be walking to Simon and Garfunkel today dressed in swimsuit and goggles, while thinking of my lovely brother in hospital.
I am reading a book Jacqui gave me called Gutsy Women written by Hillary and Chelsea Clinton. Yesterday I read the chapter on Anne Frank and certainly made me consider that our "lockdown" is nothing like theirs was.!!!
Lots love to all
Be with you on Monday

30th March

Gladys

My lovely Brian is out of hospital, still needing to take care and hospital almost certain no Covid 19. However he has to isolate even at home from Maureen for the next 7 days! Lots of love to them both.
Hope you are all refreshed after the day off yesterday ! Alright I know several of you still exercised. I did not, so today I am walking to something a bit more upbeat ABBA .

I am thinking of Paula Ratcliffe running a marathon and I am wearing running shorts vest and a sweat band. However, I shall not be stopping by the side of the garden, should I need a wee!!
Off at 9.30am
At least sun is shining this morning and no gales.
We can do it - chins up etc etc.
Gladysxxx

Jacqui

I don't think it was a wee......... Just setting off round the block with Dave.

<u>31st March</u>

Gladys

The children across the road went round the cul de sac yesterday and chalked a picture on the pavement outside each house. It is lovely (unfortunately got washed away with the rain) but I was delighted to see my butterfly.
Today I am going all French! I am wearing black skirt, striped top, beret and fishnet tights while playing " Paris after dark"

Just wondering if the reason this self distancing seems to be working is because we British have always been good at queueing. !!!!

1st April

Gladys

Hi, everyone, slightly different today as I am not walking to music as I intend to do my walking outside in the close and even go on an adventure to the post box in St Johns rd. Think neighbours would object if I put music on so loud I could hear it in the road. However I shall be keeping up my immaculate attire and, so as not to disappoint the neighbours, I shall be wearing a pink leotard very similar to the one the young mum opposite was wearing doing her exercises yesterday!!
Those of you who started with me at the beginning, we have been doing this for 2 weeks today - well done to everyone 🌸 🌸
Much love xx

<u>2nd April</u>

Gladys

Thought you would enjoy this from Maureen!
My missive is a bit early today because I shall be
walking round my lounge from 9am listening to
a "simulcast" on radio 2. —5 radio stations,
including radio 1 and radio 2, 6 music, 1extra ,
Asian network, are doing a request programme
singalong. So will be a variety of music and may
be a bit of fun. Anyway, I shall walk for the
usual 1/2 hour. Could be listening to music I
don't usually hear! The dress code today is ......
trousers and white polo neck sweater. I know
boring uh?
Lots of love xxx
P.s. Glad you are wearing a few pairs black
knickers, Maureen, but doesnt it get a bit hot ???
I presume you mean with nothing else !

Maureen R

I hope you all enjoy this as much as I did. I will be walking with you this morning and mixing in my P.E exercises as usual. Today I might add in some weights. Not dressing exotically as I know at least one of you is. The competition is too much for me and the nearest I get to sexy at the moment is a few pairs of black knickers. (Not today though.) Keep well and smiling through. Remember we are British and will never be defeated. Well not yet anyway. X

I'm normally a social girl
I love to meet my mates
But lately with the virus here
We can't go out the gates.

You see, we are the 'oldies' now
We need to stay inside
If they haven't seen us for a while
They'll think we've upped and died.

They'll never know the things we did
Before we got this old
There wasn't any Facebook
So not everything was told.

We may seem sweet old ladies
Who would never be uncouth
But we grew up in the 60s -
If you only knew the truth!

There was sex and drugs and rock 'n roll
The pill and miniskirts
We smoked, we drank, we partied
And were quite outrageous flirts.

Then we settled down, got married
And turned into someone's mum,
Somebody's wife, then nana,
Who on earth did we become?

We didn't mind the change of pace
Because our lives were full
But to bury us before we're dead
Is like a red rag to a bull!

So here you find me stuck inside
For 4 weeks, maybe more
I finally found myself again
Then I had to close the door

It didn't really bother me
I'd while away the hour
I'd bake for all the family
But I've got no bloody flour!

Now Netflix is just wonderful
I like a gutsy thriller
I'm swooning over Idris
Or some random sexy killer.

At least I've got a stash of booze
For when I'm being idle
There's wine and whiskey, even gin
If I'm feeling suicidal!

So let's all drink to lockdown
To recovery and health
And hope this bloody virus
Doesn't decimate our wealth.

We'll all get through the crisis
And be back to join our mates
Just hoping I'm not far too wide
To fit through the flaming gates!

3rd April

Gladys

It is my super sister in law Maureen's birthday today. They are on their 5th day of self distancing- happy birthday Maureen, only another 2 days to go!!
Tom and I had several great holidays in France with Maureen and Brian so today's theme is French again!
Today I am wearing culottes and a shawl and have my knitting ready while walking to Les Miserables. (Our holidays were anything but miserable!!)
Did you go out and clap last night? I actually managed not to nod off and went to the front door. There were 5 households out clapping and we all yelled across to each other as well. It was lovely. Xx

Jo

Puff puff puff...just done my walking on a compact stepping machine I bought a few years ago and have neglected.

Interesting news on FaceTime with Ang and Ian last night: Ian said, "Uncle Brian has now come out."   Love to all, Jo

Gladys

This day and age you can own up to anything-
even my extensive wardrobe! You knew that
stepping machine would come in handy, Jo.
Well done.
Lots love Gladysxx

4th April

Gladys

After the less than joyful walk "les miserables"
yesterday- decided I need a bit more joy and
glamour! So today I am wearing a strapless
midnight blue evening dress, white gloves,
pearls and a diamond tiara - walk(zt)ing to
Rupert Parker Double Harp! I am a little
concerned about the stiletto heels for 1/2 hour!
Have a lovely day tomorrow in the promised
sunshine and be careful of those sausages on
your virtual bbq- make sure they are cooked
through!
Be with you all again on Monday
Lots love xxxx

6th April

Gladys

I know many of you spent several hours working in the garden yesterday, so you need to exercise those limbs today!
As an homage to the nhs, including my nephew Thomas who will be working at the Nightingale hospital, I am wearing a nurses uniform today and walking to Neil Diamond. Of course my uniform is a la carry on films. Think Barbara Windsor (did I hear someone say Hattie Jaques!!!!)And if anyone does remember I shall be carrying a daffodil!!
Personally thought the Queens speech was good.
A new week everyone
Lots of love xxxxx

7th April

Gladys

Today I am walking for our men.
First a very happy birthday to my David
Thinking particularly of our men who are no
longer with us - Tom Kelvin Terry Ted John
Dick Brian - with love
My 2 lovely brothers Brian and Bob
You will have seen the video from Ian yesterday
to say he will be walking a marathon round his
garden supporting Kevin Webber and prostate
cancer. Ian set off at 8 am and of course I am
very proud of him, so for my walk today I am
wearing my prostate cancer t shirt- as worn at
last years March for Men in Stratford-while
listening to cd of favourite love songs. I am also
wearing a medal.
Good luck Ian
Lots of love to everyone
Xxxx

8th April

Gladys

Thinking of Wendy at home with her son Peter who is exhibiting signs of the virus. Lots of love and get well soon Peter.
Well done Ian, yesterday- amazing achievement. I havent reached a marathon yet with my walking every day- will let you know when I do!!! Maybe I am hampered by my wardrobe! Today I am harping back to the sixties, wearing the tiniest of mini skirts and my hair in a Mary Quant bob, listening to "Cilla" while walking. We have reached the 3 weeks mark today since I started sending out e mails. Just let me know if it is all too much and you would prefer not to receive them each morning. I quite understand- visions of me in some of my outfits could put you off your breakfasts!
Much love to all, keep in touch
Xxxx

Gladys

Forgive me if the e mail is a bit breathless, but for today's walk I have spent the past 1/2 hour pouring myself in to a pair of black leather skin-tight trousers, a blond wig and high heels a la Olivia Newton John in Grease. The only thing I don't remember about Olivia is that there were any overhanging bumps ! I have had to make sure that all my toilet requirements were taken care of as there is no way I shall be able to stop half way or for that matter quickly at the finish of my walk! Of course, my cd music today is Grease! I shall be setting off as soon as I end the e mail today- there is no way I can sit down wearing this!!
Jill has joined our group from today , I did warn you about the light-hearted e mails
Jill didn't I??

Jill

Wow, my imagination is on overtime, certainly makes me look very dull. Black trousers and a blue and grey animal print top. To make matters worse was going to listen to Bryn Tervil. Well I am new to this. Stay safe x

Janet

Very funny! Tears of laughter here and the description brilliant. A hard act to follow I think. What a good job it's a warm sunny day and not a damp wet one!! Hopefully will be easier to remove at end of walk!! Be safe all xx

10th April

Gladys

After the effort of putting on and taking off the leather trousers yesterday, I have decided on a more demure, comfortable outfit today. Remember the 50's? Today I am wearing a flared dress with a hooped/ frilly petticoat, short white gloves and shoes with kitten heels. (the hoops could be a problem when you sat down and the dress/ petticoat went up at the front). My cd is Dreamboats and petticoats- lots of different artists-Paul Anka, Bobby Darin, Lonnie Donegan, Elvis etc.

Also remember the only shop open on Good Friday used to be the Bakers in the morning so you could buy hot cross buns- dont eat too many today!!

Stay home, daresay the Great Escape will be on the tv!!   Lots of love xxx

11th April

Gladys

As you know I record the steps I walk in my 1/2 hour every day, and my fitbit also records the distance. Yesterday it showed I had clocked up 26.5 miles a marathon in 3 weeks. I know some of you are exercising, walking, cycling much further so a big clap to all of us. I wonder how far it will be by the end of lockdown!
Today I am walking wearing a white bunny rabbit suit, with big floppy ears and big feet, while carrying a basket of Easter eggs to hide round the garden. Listening to radio 2 as I shall be mostly outside and not hear a cd.
No e mail tomorrow as it is Sunday. A very happy Easter to everyone.
I shall be walking round the garden looking for Easter eggs(remember my age, I shall have forgotten where I hid them!!)
Much love to you all
Stay safe
Stay in
Gladysxx

12th April

Gladys

Much love and hugs for Easter to you and all your families! Had my first chocolate for over 3 weeks! Unfortunately couldnt quite leave it until today, so had some of the 80th bar you gave me Maureen and Brian, on Thursday! Still it was Maundy Thursday so technically Easter! Today have started on the Easter egg I bought for someone else!!
At least we have some lovely weather , so enjoy, and really looking forward to seeing everyone in the not too distant future.
Stay safe, keep well
Keep in touch
So happy that I saw you in February
Hugs hugs hugs xxx

Brian

Dear all
Wishing you all a very happy Easter
Loving all your e-mails. Outfits,Birds, Flowers and bikes.
Keep well stay safe. Love to all your families.
Bob: "Lets be careful out there" I think that was Hill Street Blues (they don't make them like that

anymore. A great series) can't recall the name of the cop who said it. Do I get 1/2 point?
Much love
M&B xx

Bob

Rather surreal for me so far. On thursday out on bike saw 2 shiny mountain bikes parked outside a Sainsburys Local completely unlocked .
Thought rather silly
even in a nice area ,as I knew to my cost . But as I may need sugar soon went in store . Quite crowded though . realised I silly too. Didn't need it that much
if at all. As you know I sweet enough already so came straight again. Saw 2 police, 1 man and 1 woman just getting on the bikes. I didn't like to ask whether
they the distance patrol and why in pairs. Yesterday in the garden sitting in the sun got too hot - in the middle of April, so moved back under the tree.
But of course no leaves meant no shade. Later as I setting out on my walk (I try to alternate days cycling or walking) I saw a woman wander into the close
with a cat - on a lead. Does it beg ? I asked .What do you mean ? her reply. Does it sit up

and beg like a dog ? I said . It's A CAT she pointed out.

Ah well female logic ? But there is still humour about. I then had my walk past a house which has 2 lifesize statues of Great Dane dogs outside.

This time they were wearing face masks, I took a photo - from a safe distance of course

Our first Easter eggs ! Were they shaped icing sugar mixes with some chocolate coating ? as I fondly remembered or were they actually just real eggs

painted chocolate ? as I thought one of you said more realistically.

Anyway take care out there. (Who said that in what 70's American Cop Series ?)

Love Bob

13th April

Gladys

After bingeing on chocolate(not had any for 4 weeks!) and the change in the weather today, I decided I need something to to encourage and spur me on, so what could be better than Freddie Mercury.

So today I am wearing a white sleeveless vest, white trousers, yellow short military jacket and of course a black moustache and listening to Queen while walking.

It is 35 years since live aid so all those who were there/ listening will be in the same position as us -missing family and friends etc.

So keep at it -a new week

WE ARE THE CHAMPIONS

Much love to all

Gladysxx

14th April

Gladys

I have been thinking positive and remembering some of the lovely holidays I have had over the years and of course the ones still to come! Today it was the fantastic holidays I had in Australia so I am wearing a pair of knee length khaki shorts, khaki shirt, sturdy lace up boots and of course a hat with corks dangling round the edges, listening to a dreamtime cd bought in Cairns. So many wonderful memories, but maybe one that sticks out is travelling back from Monkey Mia to Perth (850k) and realising that

with the petrol gauge showing empty , there are not nearly as many service stations along that road as there are on the M25!!
Love to all
Xxx

Jacqui

Think you may have learned a few new swear words from your daughter as she responded to your son in laws comment not to worry we were in the RAC!!!!!!

15th April

Gladys

For those who have been with me from the start, today marks the end of the 4th week of our 'walks' and my Narnia cupboard is nowhere near empty of clothes yet! It is also exactly half way through April, so time is passing. I have decided to wear my Morris dancing outfit today, trousers tucked in socks, with bells just below the knees, white shirt with cross bands and my straw hat with flowers. Of course, I have my stick in my hand to pound on the floor. I shall be

thinking of being English and getting through this while listening to English country music. Sun shining
Xx

16th April

Gladys

Today I am wearing a Bo Peep puffed sleeved dress, red shoes, make up and a red bow in my hair - my 'friend' Grayson Perry's alter ego Claire. He is hosting a weekly - Graysons Art Club from his studio , starting this evening, but unfortunately he is unwell and the start has been postponed until 27th April channel 4 8pm. However I shall try to get out in the garden with my paper and pencils and see what occurs. (please stop laughing those of you who have seen my art attempts before) On the 27th the theme is portraits so I am not sure whose portrait I shall be doing!!

Janet

You kept that outfit up your sleeve. I trust the lipstick is the exact match for the red Bow! I do fear that any nesting birds in the vicinity could be alarmed by such an outrageous outfit, and

I'm sure You will be very quiet when putting pencils to paper....no Elvis blaring in background please.
Heard nephew Thomas is returning to the font line on Sunday. I'm sure we all wish him and his colleagues the best of luck
in the mammoth task they have. Saucepan lid and wooden spoon at the ready for tonight's appreciation noises...even more poignant now!
Be safe all xx

17th April

Gladys

After yesterday's rather flamboyant outfit and the time it took me to take off the makeup and false eyelashes, I have gone for a somewhat less flamboyant outfit today! I am wearing a prison uniform complete with arrows and carrying a ball and chain!! I shall be listening to O Brother Where art thou? The main reason for this cd is to remember all the good times we have had at various times, Andy on guitar, Ian on banjo and my 2 nephews Steven and Simon on their guitars. I am so looking forward to the next time there is a get together and we sing our hearts out!

The other reason is that O brother etc reminds me of George Clooney and it always does me good to be reminded of George Clooney.
Just hope the ball and chain doesn't get too heavy!!
Sun shining again, that can't be bad either.
Xxx

Ian

A very hurriedly put together banjo rendition (a loose description, other than it's on the banjo) to accompany Mum with her ball and chain. Please forgive the mistakes.
Mother, where art thou...

Colin

Bravo Ian! And Gladys too.
After the frivolity of yesterday's outing inspired by Grayson Perry's. (That House! How do you did he ever get planning permission?) I think today you have been inspired Gladys. Did the thought of George have anything to do with this I wonder?
I shall think of you always now stumbling along on the chain gang (Cool Hand Luke and Paul Newman - even better looking if you ask me) gasping for water. Please stay away from the

boiled eggs for a while though - you know it
makes sense.
Colin x

18th April

Gladys

Rather a dull morning - did we have any much-
needed rain?
So today I am thinking about some Saturday
evenings, of a certain era, as they used to be! I
am wearing a flared padded shoulders dress and
a very curly perm wig and going to the "Copper
Pot" for disco, I shall be listening to cd non stop
party album (Dexys midnight Runners, Right
Said Fred etc),
No walk tomorrow but I shall be back Monday.
Enjoy your fantasy Saturday evening wherever
you go.
Xx

Ian
Happy times at the police club. I remember well
Mum's curly perm. Or perhaps it was natural?

20th April

Gladys

Forgive my ramblings today. Hope you had a good Sunday, as always lots of time for thinking. My thoughts were particularly, where would we be without the internet and www at this time? I know we are all going to turn into continentals and hug and kiss everybody we see, I long to hug my family when they come with my shopping and I even longed to hug the RAC man when he came to put a new battery in my car, but until then we are lucky to have this. The internet was only invented in 1983 by Kahn and Cerf (had to look this up) then Tim Berners Lee invented www. in 1990 How wonderful and lucky we are, e mails, texts, FaceTime, (see so many of my friends and family) and for many Facebook. And yesterday another piece of magic for me when I joined a Culhane zoom , 7 families all on one screen, and we did a Ben quiz. It was so good, I came last by the way. But enough of my ramblings and back to today with some nostalgia, I found and am wearing my shocking pink hot pants and knee length boots and thinking of THE BEATLES. My cd today. I had a shock last year when watching a quiz show on tv and a youngster didn't know who the

Beatles were!
A new week- We can work it out
Gladysxx

Jacqui

If not already suggested, 'I am the Walrus' after all the chocolate I've had!!!!

Ian

*I enjoyed Mum's Beatles reference at the end -
We Can Work it Out.
Maybe with all technology around, 'Help' might
be another one?
Challenge - any other Beatles songs you can
think of relevant for the current situation?*

Janet

*Yes! A challenge! I feel fine, so thought I'd take
a walk down The long and winding road via
Penny Lane to Strawberry Fields. On the way I
met Eleanor Rigby, who said she was getting by
With a little help from my friends. Hoping this
will all be over When I'm sixty-Four so that we
can all Come Together at last!!*

Gladys

I think you win Jan! I think 'With a little help from my friends' is the one we all need. Good challenge Ian, hope we can come up with some more appropriate ones. Don't think Sergeants Peppers lonely hearts club band will be of any use!!

21st April

Gladys

It is Queen Elizabeth's birthday today and so to mark the occasion I am dressed in the (usual) 'opening of parliament' regalia. I am wearing a long white jewel encrusted dress, an ermine trimmed cloak and a crown and I am listening to the last night of the proms. I know it should be the National Anthem but standing still rather defeats the object. I appreciate that it may be rather warm and there is a danger the crown could fall off my head but it is the bl...y corgis nipping at my ankles I am more worried about! Happy birthday your majesty!!
Xxxx

Ian

Love the idea of you exercising by standing still to the national anthem!

Jill

I would curtsy but afraid my knees might lock and I would then fall at your feet....there's a thought. You would then have to step over me putting your crown more at risk of toppling off.

Instead I will wish your Majesty happy birthday, good health and long may you reign xx

<u>22nd April</u>

Gladys

Yesterday Maureen and I should have gone to see the Tutankhamen exhibition in London. 😩 So today I am thinking all things Egyptian and I am dressed in a long white dress with a gold necklace, belt, and thong sandals. My wig is jet black with a fringe and I have a gold hat- think Elizabeth Taylor as Cleopatra. (the eye shadow and mascara has taken me hours) I am being borne down the Nile on the royal barge rowed by galley slaves while walking for 30minutes , difficult in the sandals.

Just a reminder that it is now 5 weeks since we started the daily walks/exercise!

Well done, keep it up,

Gladysxx

23rd April

Gladys

Subject: Bore Da!

Today I shall be walking for another country of the UK, Wales! I am wearing a black skirt with an apron over the top a cape and a tall black hat with a bow that ties under the chin and listening to Bryn Terfel (have a slight problem here as the only cd of Bryn that I have is Christmas carols/songs- just hope this doesnt mean it could go on until Christmas).

There are several among our group with links to Wales, I , and of course my brothers and sister have a great grandfather , Robert Edwards, who was born in Betwys Coed, Brian and Maureen have son and family who live in Wales, jill and Bryan(who after 91 years has never lost his welsh accent) and of course Eileen who moved to Cwm Bran only last year.

Just think Snowdon is 0.67 miles high and we have walked that several times over since we started!!
Xxx

Brian

Maureen thought she would keep to the Welsh theme and has just finished her walk dressed in her traditional Welsh costume.
However, she did encounter a few problems with the miners hat/ lamp slipping over her eyes and the pick axe proved heavier than she had thought also the boots slowed her down. But she still managed her 20 mins slog and after her scrub up has kept up the tradition up by wearing a few daffodils in her hair. All this whilst singing " Hi ho Ho ho and off to work we go " in a welsh accent. I'm sure our Welsh grandchildren, Johnathan & Katie, would have been very proud. Speak to you soon.
Much love
M&B xx

24th April

Gladys

Overlooked the fact that it was St Georges day and Shakespeare's birthday yesterday! How could I forget?? So, decided I would commemorate the 2 anniversaries today. Was going to wear my dragon costume but realised it is not sensible to walk round the house and garden breathing fire, so turned to Shakespearean characters. After much thought decided that the ruff , tights and codpiece not only uncomfortable, but also not a good look! So, have settled for the character, that best suited me, doesn't need a wig or makeup, just a tall pointed black hat and cape. - one of the three witches from Macbeth.

So that I don't feel too miserable am listening to Tom Jones, missed him yesterday (thanks Jan). Xxx

Janet
Ha ha!....and the song of the day was " It's not unusual!!" ....well you always exercise in strange attire, the neighbours must be used to it by now!! You could have gone as Delilah, so could be worse! Stay safe XX

Gladys

Subject: Another week over!

It has been a rather full on week this week! That crown kept falling off my head on Tuesday, the gold thong sandals were hell to walk with, and trying to learn the words to Sospan Bach in Welsh while walking did my head in(incidentally its worth a look at the English translation and ask yourself why??). Then forgetting Shakespeare's birthday finished the week off!

So today to end the week I am being rather subdued. I am wearing a pair of dungarees, check shirt and walking while listening to the Platters (smoke gets in your eyes etc).

Keep calm, have a good weekend and I will be with you refreshed, again on Monday.

Xxxx

Colin

Gladys it always brightens my day when I receive the email about of your daily exercise in costume.

I do wonder whether your extensive wardrobe of clothes might become exhausted as the lock down goes on.

*I would hate for you to have to repeat yourself
and cause embarrassment (God forbid).
Thanks for making me smile each day.*

Jo

*My friend has just finished Quarton and loved it.
She asked me where Ian got his imagination.
These past few weeks I think I am just
discovering where some of it comes from!!!*

Joxx

Jill

*Sospan Bach is the anthem for the Scarletts
(Llanelli) Rugby team, the top of the rugby poles
each have an upside down black saucepan.
Llanelli locals are called 'saucepan'. You
managed to get Bry thinking, he 'sang' it and
actually remembered the second versus. Painful
as Bry cannot sing.
Thanks for brightening up our week.
Take care and stay safe.
Love from us both.
Xxx*

Brian

Dear Glad,

How soon you forget your Welsh roots . The little sauce pan is of course a favourite Welsh nonsense verse and is widely sung at many an occasions all over Wales.

Your Great Grandfather would be very disappointed with you if he thought you might be disrespecting our Welsh heritage.

However, it did get me thinking about our Welsh connection with Great Grandad Edwards coming down from Betwsys Coed to London to help lay the tram lines all those years ago and now (I believe) with the last of the Edwards' to carry on the name being is left to our Jonathan back in Wales again.

We had many a good time spent in Wales with our Jonathan & Katie visiting some of the many castles that Wales has to offer but best of all our many trips to (Gavin & Stacy's) Barry Island. I recall spending many a happy afternoon seeing them playing on sand. It was only after one of these trips that I had to say " you can only have another 15mins as we have to get you home" to which they both replied in unison "Do we have to say another 15mins" that we realised perhaps Barry didn't hold that magic for them anymore.

Their nearest town to them is that lovely town Caerphilly which got me thinking perhaps a little Welsh Caerphilly quiz to help you brush up on your Welsh might be appropriate for the weekend.

It has been an exciting week for us, with the arrival of my much awaited Jig Saw puzzle and Maureen's knighting needles so we are looking forward to many fun filled afternoons. The other event was the excitement of receiving our Tesco online delivery. Although the Einchcomb's have been tending to our needs it is was nice to be able to be a little independent now and again. Well birthdays played a part in the morning walks last week with celebrating the Queens and Shakespeare's birthday and it was also nice to remember Karan's, David's 30th and Philip's Anna's birthday as we strolled round and hope they were able to celebrate in their own way.

Speak to you soon

Much Love to one and all. Have a lovely safe weekend.

m&b xxx

Gladys

As we enter the 6th week of lockdown(is it only that???). I feel we are all superheroes so today I am wearing my batman suit. Don't think Christian Bale, Adam West, etc more Del-boy from Only fools and horses! I find the bat mask quite fetching and covering many wrinkles, looking forward to the cape flowing behind me as I walk, but wearing pants on the outside of my clothes, not a good look especially for an 80 year old!
We are all heroes in our way and we shall continue to be.
Lots of love xxxx

P.s. as you know Grayson Perry is one of my art heroes, and for anyone interested he is starting a series on Channel 4 at 8 pm this evening which looks very interesting.

Ian

Bearing in mind the exercise theme is Superheroes today, I shall be going on my exercise bike later dressed as my mum.

(I think that puts me - or keeps me - ahead, Jacqui, in the sibling challenge for favourite child)
Ian x

28th April

Gladys

It almost seems as if we are isolated on a desert island at times, so I have been listening to some desert island discs programmes and for today I am wearing my pirate costume. The black hat with the skull and crossbones, the kerchief, and eye patch. Unfortunately the parrot keeps squawking and won't sit still on my shoulder (unless I do a Monty python!) and I am not too keen on walking for 1/2 hour with a wooden peg leg!
Shiver me timbers
Xxx
Has got me thinking- what discs would you choose?
Please share

Ian

Tracks for a desert island? Now that's a good question. Needs some thought so I'll get back to you on that.
What about the rest of you? Anyone chosen already? What else are we allowed, Mum?

Maureen R

I hope you are not cast away too long as I would miss you. Facetime probably hasn't reached your island yet. The disc I think is most appropriate in those circumstances is "Stranger on the Shore." See you later, hopefully, at our virtual coffee morning. M.X.

<u>29th April</u>

Gladys

Some of you may have noticed that this missive is a bit earlier than usual. That is because, against the advice of my family, I am going on an expedition after 6 weeks cooped up indoors. I am wearing a pith helmet, safari jacket, knee length shorts and of course hiking boots. I am taking my rucksack containing, hand gel, wipes,

6ft long walking stick and face mask. I understand I am likely to encounter bi peds but if I keep a distance of 6feet between us, should cause no problem especially during the hour 9-10am when it is only the older members of the tribe that are out.

I leave you with this quote "I am just going outside and may be some time" although I am hoping I don't suffer the same fate as Captain Oates!!

Look out Tesco, here I come!!

Xx

Edna

Have you survived the expedition how brave you are I did two short walks in the rain just because I enjoy walking in the rain sorry no punctuation on my screen!   I liked Grayson Perry but needed more art. 6 o'clock; must hear the news Boris now has 6 children!! Love Edna x

Colin

Gladys that is the funniest thing I have read in ages.

I felt just the same (cooped up) prior to going on my expedition to the hospital a couple of days ago but I wasn't as well prepared as you seem to be.

I don't think I could have got away with the knee length shorts given the state of my legs.

I am sure you are back now sitting in your comfy chair with a very agreeable gin and tonic and a nice biscuit or two waiting by your side.

You deserve it! X

<u>30th April</u>

Gladys

Safely back with supplies from my expedition yesterday and so today I am walking in full highland dress and thinking of our friends in Scotland (referendum what referendum?). While walking I shall be playing the bagpipes, much appreciated by the neighbours and looking forward to haggis and fried mars bar later.

Congratulations to Captain Tom on his wonderful fundraising and his 100 birthday. We have been exercising each day for over 6 weeks now and if you would like to put that exercising to good use by raising some money for charity, checkout Prostate cancer uk Move for Men , or any other charity, they all need help. I have signed up and sponsored myself to walk for 1/2 hour every day for 30 days . I am already doing that but I shall be donating to prostate cancer the money I would have spent going out for coffee/ scone at least twice a week. You were all so generous in February at my birthday celebrations and I can't thank you enough, but if you did feel that you wanted to put all the energy you are using exercising to good use, then check out the web site. (it doesn't have to be walking!!)

Thank you

Much love, sun is shining

Gladysxx

1st May

Gladys

Had a bit if a dilemma choosing todays costume!
Should I go with the International Workers day
garb sing the Internationale and carry a red flag
or choose the traditional Spring flowers dress
and wear my crown of flowers while walking?
In the end I decided on the latter and will sing
traditional English folk songs, tra la la. After all
it seems such a shame not to dance round the
10foot Maypole I took hours to erect in the
middle of the lawn yesterday.

Lets hope by the time it comes round to say
Rabbits or Pinch punch first day of the month,
next time, we shall actually be able to say them
in person.

Xxx

Edna

*Would be a treat to see you in your gear. Am
just going to see if my car will start it has had a
long rest . Went to Sainsbury's in the back of
Julie's car I really enjoyed the ride .Tesco are*

delivering tomorrow all my naughty treats
.Enjoy May Day cheers Edna x

2nd May

Gladys

Subject: Coach trips
Every two months a thick envelope would arrive
through the post from Mercury travel with
details of forthcoming trips and Maureen Edna
Shirley and I would spend time choosing which
ones we would book. The next newsletter was
due now! Who knows when and if there will be
another one.
The last trip was on March 8th to Cliffs Pavilion
Southend, when Daphne came, to see Swan
Lake performed by the Russian Ballet. So today
for my walk, I am wearing a white tutu, pointe
ballet shoes and a feather headdress. Think more
Dawn French than D'Arcy Bussell.!
I leave you with that image for the weekend.
Be with you again Monday
Xxx

Ian

Good one for Dad too - he so loved ballet!

Brian

Dear Glad,

I said to Maureen that you were walking in your "tutu" costume and suggested she could do the same. It is a long time since she dressed up in her little ballet outfit and wondered if she would still look as fetching as the last time she wore it.

However, you can imagine my disappointment as I looked out the patio doors and saw her dressed an "Anglican Cleric". Somehow this did not have the same effect. So as I removed the padding from my ballet tights thought perhaps a bible class might be in order to cleanse the mind of any lecherous thoughts.

Talking of coach trips I always remember our Mum with her front seats. And of course you all leaving me behind at the half way coach stop and the coach having to turn back in order to pick me up.
We can only hope is not too long before we get over this and can once again look forward to getting out and about.
Much love
m&b xx

Gladys

Now that is clever, at my advanced age it took me a while to get it!

Yes, I must admit I can see the attraction of the front seats on coaches and whenever Maureen and I go on our Mercury trips, we always get the front seats if we can. Sometimes means pushing past those on walking frames or wheelchairs to get to the coach first.

I always remember when we went to Germany with mum and dad on a coach trip, we managed to book the front seats for them and they were delighted, except that they seemed to sleep for most of the journeys out in the coach as they were so full of energy during the evenings, dancing etc.

Have you been out at all? As I said I did go to Tesco, was extremely anxious and spent as long wiping everything down when I got home as I did in the shop. I think we are going to be very nervous until a vaccine is ready. I have taken car for a run and think I shall take it for a run to Ians and social distance myself in his garden and have a chat sometime soon. Is this allowed? Only if I am getting shopping I suppose, so perhaps call at Tesco first. I dont walk round the streets near me, just houses, and sooner just walk round house/ garden like I do every day. Oh dear it is a dilemma.

Anyway chin up , keep smiling
Take care and keep well and safe
Lots love xxxx

Bob

I am doing Tesco again tomorrow . Forgot it
officially BH so hope they'll still give me and
the grannies priority .
When I went on a bus once with mum she asked
me if I wanted to sit up the front.
I was then aged about 40
Love Bob

4th May

Gladys

As you will know today is star wars day
May the fourth be with you!
So I have decided to go for a bit of glamour and
wear my princess Leia costume, long sleeves,
high neck white dress with a belt and carrying a
light saber. I have had a bit of trouble sorting
the hair 'bangs' on each side of my head and did
consider that my Chewbacca costume would
have been easier and would not have needed
much make up.
A new week, who knows what it will bring,
Much love ♡

<u>5th May</u>

Gladys

Today is Toms birthday and he would have been 85! He was a great fan of the original Star Trek so in his honour I am dressed as Captain James T Kirk of the Starship Enterprise. I am wearing a long sleeved yellow t shirt with an enterprise logo, black trousers tucked into short Black boots and carrying my phaser set to stun! I am sending you all the Vulcan hand greeting, which incidentally Tom could never do, and I shall boldly go where no man has gone before(well, the end of my garden,).
Beam me up Scottie,
Live long and prosper
Xxxx

Janet

Love it! I'm sure Tom would approve of your attire and theme for today's walk. Never a fan, I might get somewhere near the space theme by being on a flying bike from ET...an experience never forgotten from a visit to Universal Studios in Florida. May the force be with you all... stay safe !xx

Gladys

Today's costume has been the most difficult so far -Dr. Who. I had tucked the Dalek in the far corner of the wardrobe, not wanting to be reminded of the times spent hiding behind the settee on a Saturday. After a struggle I managed to negotiate the doors of the wardrobe and struggled down the stairs and out into the garden. I shall have to inspect any damage to furniture and paintwork after my 'walk'. It is quite comfortable, once inside, and I am considering it the ultimate anti covid 19 protection gear that I might wear next time I go to Tesco. However I now realise there is a design fault in that once inside I would be unable to reach anything from the shelves! Still, maybe if I keep yelling Exterminate, exterminate, it might just do that to the virus! Today is the last of my sci fi costumes, but I must give a shout out to the greatest living sci fi writer, he has the initials IH, and to say to his millions of fans all over the world that the sequel to the Quarton will be available very soon !!
It might seem that we are on another planet sometimes, but keep safe and keep well.
Xxxx

7th May

Gladys

Today is the turn of Northern Ireland! I am dressed in a green tunic and a pointed hat and holding a shillelagh in my hand (that is not a euphemism!) while listening to Irish Eyes. I am desperately hoping that the pot of gold at the end of the rainbow contains the vaccine!
Xxx

Brian

Dear Glad and All,
Today Maureen decided continue with the Irish theme and is dressed in her little all green Leprechaun outfit carrying her little hammer in one hand and shoe in the other (a lot of cobblers really but that's Irish traditions for you) accompanied by Val Doonican singing Paddy Mcginty's Goat.
* She said she was going out to kiss the Blarney Stone (I don't think that was a euphemism either but then again ….......).*
""I like you I do so hope that pot of gold at the end of the rainbow contains that vaccine."" and the sooner the better for all of us.
However, Maureen being of certain height and dressed all in green, and with the grass being

left to grow for a while……. I think I will give it another half hour and if she's not returned go in after her. It's just as well St. Patrick got rid of all those snakes or we could be in real trouble.

Hope you have a lovely time tomorrow with your neighbours for VE day remembrance street do. (I wonder if your next door neighbours will join you all) We can't get over how great it is of them to come up with such a lovely idea. Will you be going in costume?   Lastly what excellent news hearing from Karren regarding Frank getting the all clear from his consultant. We are so pleased for them and now that is something to celebrate.

With much love Say safe and look forward to when we can all get together again.
Love m&b xx

Maureen

Thought you might like to know that I am enjoying being part of your extended family.
Love M X

<h1 style="text-align: center;"><u>8th May</u></h1>

Gladys

Subject: V.E.day

Today, for me, is going to be the most exciting day since lockdown. It is the day of our self-distancing V.E party. We are lucky in our little Close (only 12 houses) in that no through traffic, also we are lucky that Lou, who lives opposite has sent invitations and is organising it. It seems that everyone in the Close is in favour as many of the houses have bunting flags etc. We are taking chairs food and drink 🍺 and we shall sit at the end of our driveways, all self distancing. Lou and Dan have a PA system and are organising a quiz, it will be so good, even if I just sit and nod!!!

Jan I was going to dig out my Andrews sisters American army uniform, but I am giving my wardrobe a rest today and wearing blue trousers, red top, and a red/white/blue scarf while waving my union jacks!

I shall be the only one there who can remember the war, and the street parties we went to in East Ham and Plaistow (Bob), going down the shelter we shared with the Frith family, and a part of the dismantled Morrison table falling on my ankle and having to be pushed round in a pushchair for a while !

My only wish for today would be that all of us could be together having a huge party 🎉
Whatever you do, think positive, it will be over and end, no bluebirds etc,
Lots and lots of love xxxxxxxxx

Brian

That sounds really lovely, have a great day.
Speak to you soon
Much Love m&b xxx

Gladys

Party lovely and itv anglia news here and just been interviewed ! xx

9th May

Gladys

Today I am walking in a long overcoat, dark glasses, hood and a scarf covering most of my face! This is not my anti covid19 costume, but after my appearance on anglia itv news yesterday at 6.50, I am being followed by hordes of fans requesting my autograph and agents wanting to book me for slots in the US and all over the world. But I do not want to desert you, my loyal fans, so I shall stay incognito. Yesterday was amazing, so friendly, all the neighbours were out in the close, houses decorated, flags bunting etc, tables and chairs with food and drink and we all social distanced while walking round chatting to each other. It was really great to see everyone in such a good mood. Lou who had organised it, did a little quiz and then we played a game of bingo. We were outside from 1pm- 5 ish.

How I wish you had all been here, but we will. Hope you all had as good a day as I had. Xxxxxxxxx

Maureen R

Fantastic. A lovely memory to cheer you up in a sad time. Although I don't have a video or tv appearance to show for it I had a good day too. I went to celebrate in one neighbour's front garden at 3pm then next door's drive at 6pm. Both lovely and now I know several neighbours better. X

Gladys

I knew it would cause problems when I struggled with the Dalek! Couldn't open the wardrobe door yesterday to get my latest walk costume! However, not to be outdone by a jammed door, I remembered the old curtains I had put in a bag ready to take to the hospice charity shop and got out my sewing machine, got carried away and made myself an Austrian dirndl dress a la Julie Andrews!

Does anyone know 7 Austrian children who would like sets of matching clothes made from curtains?

I have made lists of my favourite things, does not include raindrops on roses or whiskers on kittens!

If you missed Ian on radio Essex yesterday, you missed a real treat- even mentioned his mother!

Has Boris inspired you??

Keep alert,

Lots of love xxxx

P.s just in case you were worried, have managed to get the wardrobe door open!

Ian

Great outfit choice!
It used to take Jacqui and I ages going to bed
when we were kids - up and down the stairs, one
step at a time, while we sang our hearts out.
Mum and Dad at the foot, heads to one side,
nodding and smiling away...

So long, farewell... ♫♬♫
Ian

12th May

Gladys

I decided it is 'movies' week this week and
when I opened my wardrobe door, 3 costumes
were close by so had a bit of a dilemma when it
came to choosing. Actually it wasn't that
difficult- don't need a ♡ - we all have shown
how much we have those. Don't need courage-
enough said, but what I do need is a brain, mine
seems to be turning to mush- so my costume
today is the scarecrow - the straw is a bit itchy
especially in some places but I hope I will
understand things a bit better!
My main worry at the moment is Where am I
going to keep a 'lert' the PM insists we keep!

Are they going to hand them out like virus
testing kits and achieve a target of 100,00 a day?
When will I get mine? What will it eat? So you
can see my brain problem.
Actually I think the best thing to do is to click
my heels together and repeat
There's no place like home
There's no place like home
There's no place like home

13th May

Gladys

As I was putting on my Charlie Chaplin old suit,
black boots, bowler hat and moustache, I
suddenly remembered- Saturday Morning
Pictures!' As a youngster it was the highlight of
the week- walk to The Towers cinema in
Hornchurch, for a really great morning! The
cinema was always packed full of children- no
adults, except the long suffering usherettes and
the 'grumpy' manager. The noise was
tremendous! Every film was accompanied by
more noise from the audience than on the screen,
shouts, gun fire noises, whistles, and groans if
the hero dared show some sentiment to the
heroine. We had a surfeit of cowboys and
Indians, Roy Rogers, Gene Autry, , the goodies

wore white hats and the baddies wore black and the Indians were all savages! There was always cartoons and of course the likes of Laurel and Hardy, or Charlie Chaplin to make us laugh. We didn't have huge cartons of popcorn, or coke or hotdogs to eat or in fact anything. Sweets were still on ration until 1954(?). Remember there was no tv or discs so this was our entertainment. We were always a little amazed when we emerged from the dark of the cinema to find that it was light outside- and who didn't play cowboys and Indians all the way home? Forgive my rambling nostalgia- my Charlie Chaplin costume to blame- will be thinking all the time I am walking, swaying along with my walking stick.

Xxx

Jill

You forgot Hopalong Cassidy and Roy Rogers, I loved Trigger best of all.
Enjoy your walk and stay safe xx

Daphne

Lovely nostalgia. Went to Saturday morning @ Towers pics few times, as u say so very noisy. Films- remember episodes of Flash Gordon which used to give me nightmares & Shirley Temple (singing Good Ship Lollipop) Not know why but I didn't enjoy very much & only went one more time as told by friend that Shirley Temple would be at the cinema & of course gullible me believed her!!!! After the show used go home through park playing on swings &walking through woods jumping rivers (going home with wet socks after dared to jump), climbing trees & never remember it raining in summer tho it must have. No mums or dads to take us or pick us up in car - we all must have walked miles but never occurred to us to feel any fear. Woods were for exploring.

Took my then young sons to local theatre Westcliff summer holidays showed films for children twice weekly - They showed episodes of my favourite Swallows & Amazons (think they would have preferred Flash Gordon) Oh well - good luck with Charlie xx

Janet

How right you are Glad. It was the highlight of the week, and cowboys and Indians always a great favourite for us kids to play in the school holidays. Lucky enough to have a big field at the bottom of our turning then, so plenty of room to roam. I do recall the siren going off a couple of times in the middle of a great game and we were hastily ushered to the shelter by panicking Mums! I loved Roy Rogers and Trigger, his four legged friend who never let him down. When you look back, our pleasures were simple, but we had fun, and out in the fresh air, not heads down over a screen. Time to Hopalong in your Chaplin outfit. Thank goodness you didn't choose Buster Keaton.....might have hurt yourself trying to get onto surrounding rooftops! Will you be having a nice cup of Ovaltine for elevenses today? Keep safe XX

<u>14th May</u>

Gladys

Still on a movies theme today. I know many of you enjoyed thinking about Saturday morning pictures yesterday, so today it is another group of films some of you may have enjoyed over the years- James Bond. today I am walking while wearing the <u>Dr.No</u> white bikini with belt and a scabbard on the side to hold a large knife, hair dripping wet a la Ursula Andress! Hope you have had your breakfast and don't worry about my getting cold as I have left my vest on!
Hold that image
Who is the best James Bond? For me Sean!
Xxx

Ian

Good one!

(Best Bond? Sean - no contest).

<u>15th May</u>

Gladys

For my walk today I am dressed as a Southern Belle, more sedate than yesterday, long dress, parasol , Gone with the wind. As it has been movies week, I have been thinking of our Odeon SilverScreen. On a Tuesday, £3 and a coffee and a biscuit. Shirley and I used to go every week, (we saw some real 'bummers') but also some very good films and as we became more discerning Edna and Maureen joined us on occasions. I don't know if 'Gone with the Wind', nearly 4 hours long, would ever have been screened, the cinema audience are all of a certain age and the number of trips to the loo would have been phenomenal! I think the film music , Tara's theme, must rank among the best. Tomorrow is another day
Much love xxx

16th May

Gladys

Eurovision! Should have been on today! Hadn't really watched it for many years- the early years were when we all sat glued to the television(basically nothing else on that evening!) and revelled in the fact that Katy Boyle gave out the scores and we often got douze points! That is from one jury not the total. Who remembers Pearl Carr and Teddy Johnson- sing little birdie sing- we came second? Then of course there were the magic Sir Terry years and his commentaries, couldn't care less about the songs, but listening to Terry and his comments! Now of course, I understand Australia takes part in Eurovision, that is like being told there are 7 Continents when I was taught there were 5! Am I getting old ??
However, there were some really good things to come out of Eurovision- well I can think of one at least, and that is the double Whammy today. Eurovision and Movies.
Movies- a really feel good movie Mamma Mia, which I saw with Jacqui and the girls Jasmine and Poppy- embarrassed them by shouting out at the end of the film that I wanted another song! So of course Abba. I am wearing silver jumpsuit, little skull cap, high boots and a blonde wig- that's right dressed as Benny!! I don't know

which is my favourite Abba song- as you know
Tom was a fan as well- so I shall be listening to
my disc and singing along to all of them.
We can face it together as old friends do
Be with you on Monday
Look after your 'lert' xxx

Bob

*You are all obviously keen movie buffs so how
about a little quiz*

*The following are quotations from old films
(except for the last one which is my favourite
version of the most popular song ever) with
dashes for missing words or parts of words*

*Fill in the dashes together with the names of the
films and actors or characters speaking to win a
free seat at a cinema of your choice next week.*

Clue: The first two are from the same film

1. No Mr Bond I intend - - -

2. Sh-

3. You aint heard - -

4. I shot an arrow in the air it - - - - - -

5. *Infamy Infamy - - - - - - -*

6. *I could've been - -*

7. *Well nobody's -*

8. *He's not coming out. he's - - - - -*

9. *Fasten your seat belts it's going to be - - -*

10. *You know how to - dont you*

!1. *Aie----- Aie------ Aie-------   (This one is tricky)*

12. *Happy - Mister -*

In fact make that prize 2 seats

__18th May__

Gladys

Decided to start the week with a bit of glamour and am wearing that white dress, blonde wig, high heels and red lips from the Seven Year Itch! Marilyn, probably one of the few names where we don't have to say the second name to know who we mean! Trying to recreate that poster I have placed a hair dryer at a strategic point so that at various times in my walk you can imagine the skirt will be rising! (try not to imagine too much, especially the compression stockings!)

Hope you have done the movies quiz from Bob - not giving too much away if I say that the answer to the last question , involves this icon and JFK!

Have a good week

Xxxx

19th May

Gladys

Che, you might be wondering whether my icon today is Manuel from Fawlty Towers, but no it is Che Guevara. Surely that picture of his head must have been on the most t shirts in the world? Anyway I am Che today, wild hair and beret. No idea what clothes he wore as only seen him from the neck up, but must assume it is not a mini skirt and high heels, so have Khaki shirt and trousers. On looking at my reflection I think I am more Frank Spencer than Che Guevara. Hope you still have your taste and smell-

perhaps I shouldn't mention taste when writing these e mails! Viva la Revolution
Xxx

Ian

Fab!
Wasn't 'Che' a song by Charles Aznavour?

Brian

I'm like you Ian, I am always getting them confused.
Wasn't Charles Aznavour a Tenor where as I think Che Guevara was more of a Castrati.
I know one of them died whilst giving a "final farewell tour" in Bolivia.
I will try to find my Charles Aznavour T shirt and compare it to your Mum's outfit when we see the photos.
However, I can't remember Charles Aznavour leading a revolt but then again wasn't his follow hit to Che, Viva la Revolution. Or have I been laying in the sun too long?

<u>20th May</u>

Gladys

Today's icon fits in very nicely with sheet changing day! No need to raid the wardrobe, I have draped a sheet around my shoulders and then fashioned like pants to think of Ghandi. The non violent resistance is going well, (except whenever certain members of the government come on the tv and I throw something) but the fasting is really not good!

For those of you who have been with me from the beginning, today marks the end of the 9th week. As you know I have been counting the steps and distance covered during my morning walks- thank you for the fit-bit Abbey- and yesterday reached the end of my 3rd marathon. Today is another adventure for me- I am going to Hadleigh to see Maureen, outside social distancing of course and hoping my bladder holds out all the time until I get back home again.

Hottest day of the year, look after your ' lert'

Xxx

21st May

Gladys

After my adventure out yesterday, I felt as if I had travelled to the moon and back. Who can forget that night in July 1969, when we waited with baited breath to watch grainy tv pictures of Neil Armstrong setting foot on the moon? We woke Jacqui and Ian up (about 3 am?) to see it. So today I am dressed in my space suit, rather hot, the visor keeps steaming up and the lack of gravity is playing havoc with my fit-bit. Dont think will be an accurate number of steps as I keep flying up in the air!!
However I am praying that the giant leap for mankind will be the vaccine.
Fly me to the 🌛 moon
Xxx

22nd May

Gladys

Today I am dressed as Britain's first lady P.M, Margaret Thatcher. Her clothes reflected her personality-Royal blue suit with shoulder pads, matching blouse and of course THE handbag! However I must admit my thoughts of M .T are rather coloured by Spitting Image! Just want to share with you one of the many sketches on that programme.

Margaret was out for dinner with her cabinet.
Waiter- How would you like your steak madam?
M.T- rare
Waiter- What about the vegetables?
M.T- They will just have the same
Sorry xxx

23rd May

Gladys

Subject: Re: The King!
Greatest rock n roll but can't beat Frank as greatest singer! Xx

Discuss ...

Today I am dressed as Elvis, another of our icons this week who is recognised by just his first name! Probably the most well known rock n roll star (and in some peoples eyes the greatest, mine). I remember vividly when Heartbreak Hotel was released . I was doing o levels and it was the talk of the school. Had to be talk because could only listen on radiograms or pirate radio, frowned upon on bbc and teenagers

had only just been discovered! A great favourite of mine then and still is. So I am wearing white suit, flared trousers, gold belt, necklace and of course black wig, sunglasses and curled lip.
>> Elvis has just left the building
>> Stay safe, enjoy bank holiday weekend
>> Lots of love xxx

Colin

Elvis must have been a seismic shock for those around in the 50's. I was around in the 50's but was too young to know of the fuss - my dad had some great LP's by Elvis that he used to play. I particularly remember "GI Blues".
I can understand the appeal though.
Never quite sure about "Frank" for me being the greatest male vocalist.
Mum loved Mel Torme (who has an astonishingly beautiful voice) and Nat King Cole. She preferred those.
I think I agree. I would never argue with mum! But what an era for singing that was! (never forgetting the Blessed Ella)

Ian

Greatest male voice of all time? With Frankie?

Bob

Just one more :

Yes Sinatra the greatest singer but he was still responsible for My Way

Don't worry about Thank you message. The sun is shining now. Weather dull and cold here at the moment so indoors with mood to match and some spoilers. No pirate radio in the fifties (Radio Luxembourg legit). Guarantee Elvis never sang Heartbreak in that outfit - his 70's image. Obviously Chuck Berry never reached the Suffolk Borders
And Frankie ? Would that be Frankie Vaughan ?

<u>25th May</u>

Gladys

Saturday would have been cup final day so in nostalgia mood, again, I have been thinking about seeing Bob coming home on a Saturday afternoon having watched his beloved West Ham. (We could tell from the look on his face whether they had won or not). This was a time when we had to wait for football results on the radio, when young lads could go to matches on their own without fear, the only people who wore football kit were the players and there was only one cup final THE CUP FINAL.

However my 'kit' today is from a later era World cup 1966, thinking of the late great West Ham player Bobby Moore, and I am wearing white shirt, no 6, black shorts and football boots, while carrying the Jules Rimet trophy. Bit bothered about the boot studs on my wooden floors.

Hope you are having a safe good bank holiday weekend.

There was another self distancing party in the Close yesterday, it was really happy again, bingo, quiz and an extremely energetic game involving being the first to get certain items from in the house. Needless to say I did not attempt this but watching the youngsters competitiveness was so enjoyable. Feel very lucky I live here at such times

Am thinking of popping up to Durham, can get there and back in a day, oh sorry dont belong to the Government so will have to stick to the rules and do my walk round the house and garden as always.

Love to all xxx

Brian

Ho dear, Spoiler Alert!
I expect you have already heard from Bob, I
know we all watched it in Black & White but
England played the final of the world cup in
"Red" shirts. (Germany played in White). And
I'm not sure that he actually wiped his hands on
his shirt before shaking hands with HRH it was
more like a couple of dabs on the covering on
the edge of the Royal Box. Thought I would only
mention this before my brother gets in.

However, it is so lovely of you to keep the
morning walks going, (even on a Bank holiday)
we do so look forward to seeing what the next
day will bring. Pleased you were able to take
part in the Close party, it must be so lovely to
have these events. Such a great idea a lovely
occasion.

Speak to you soon
Much love   M&B xxx

Gladys

Brothers Uh? Now I have to do my walk all over
again in a RED shirt ! They think its all over - it
is now!

Ian

I'm surprised it took Mum so long to do a football related walk - footie mad, she is!

World Cup 1970 was the first one I can remember. Bobby was prominent then as well but not as successful. I can remember 'dancing' at school dance club to 'Back Home', the theme for the team.
Don't think I've seen that one on the lockdown playlist.

As for the Cummings and Goings of a certain individual (surely one of the papers has done that one?), let's hope it's the latter - out of the government.

<u>26th May</u>

Gladys

Not a name you hear often these days! But of course my icon for today is leader of the suffragettes Emmeline Pankhurst and wearing for my walk, what I think is a very attractive white long dress and feather hat with a purple(for loyalty) and green (for hope) sash, which were worn on the marches. I shan't be

throwing any stones, or ripping paintings, and not too sure about chaining myself to railings but I really should try a hunger strike after trying on last years Summer trousers.
I do have a placard which should say Votes for Women, but it has a very rude slogan with the words, Cummings, Durham, excuses, above, law etc.
Xxx

Ang

Go, sister suffragette!

Bob

I know they were featured recently but still can't remember was Emmeline the mum or daughter?

Poll today says 59% think He should get the boot Does that really mean that 41% actually think he need not %

Cummings and Going ! Has anybody else read "Diary of a Nobody " ? A real classic.

But England -white shirts 1966 ! Oh dear !

Bringing those 3 greats together though Sinatra ,Moore and Morecambe I have always thought they have the same thing in common - Timing !

Pompous note to end But at least no insults.
PS if anybody still at all interested I think the BBC are showing one of the films in my quiz this week in their classics series

Don't slow down Glad

27th May

Gladys

It was the 80th anniversary of Dunkirk yesterday, so for my last icon I shall be wearing a siren suit (young ones among us -google it) in honour of the man who, in a poll in 2002 was voted the greatest Briton of all time, Winston Churchill. (I didn't know that he had actually invented the siren suit in the 30's and had several made in various materials.)They became very popular with adults and children because of their ease putting on in an emergency and were also very warm and comfortable .Churchill was often seen wearing one during the war and it is probably the most comfortable item of clothing I have worn especially because it is very roomy!

Not having smoked for over 50 years, wont light the cigar, but I shall definitely be doing the 'V' gestures - maybe the wrong way round.
Cummings still not goings- farce!
Xxxx

P.s. my tv not working! Have engineer coming today, will be the first time anyone has been in my house since March- anxiety levels up, but cant manage without tv - i player on i pad not the same

28th May

Gladys

Today I am dressed in black tights, multicoloured leotard, antennae and a beautiful pair of gossamer wings. In our Close of 12 houses, over the past weeks, I have been lucky enough to have attended 2 (self distancing) parties with the neighbours. Also, I have received shouts, waves, notes, painting, drawings on the pavement all of which involved butterflies, hearts from the 3 primary school age children, Lacey, Jensen and Emilie. Yesterday morning when I opened the front door there was a painted stone with my name and a butterfly. All these have really lifted my spirits and made me smile.

The wings are very delicate and long so I shall
flutter carefully round the garden.
Keep flying
Lots of love xxx

Ian

That's so lovely to have such good neighbours.
2 further references flutter into my mind - both
very good, but in different ways.
Butterflies - Wendy Craig (worth seeing if it's on
Netflix or Amazon Prime)
Papillon - Henri Charriere

29th May

Gladys

I make no apologies whatsoever for my costume
today. I am wearing a wooden sandwich board-
and carrying a loud hailer. The sequel to
Quarton is being launched today and I am urging
everyone to buy it. (I am not biased in any
way). After being in lockdown for so many
weeks and self isolating/ distancing, what you
and all your many friends and relatives need is a
fresh off the press book. Spend some of the
money you have saved on not going out etc, to

help send this latest book to the top of the best sellers chart.

We are having a virtual book launch later this evening and there is a video made by Joe that you can get on Facebook. I am sure Ian will post links etc. about how to get the book

Good luck Ian, its great. Xxxxxxxx

Bob

At last the answers you have been breathlessly waiting for if I can finish by tonight,

First to any others who think they can wing it ,the answer, Glad of, some Bond film to a question asking which film had a quotation beginning No Mr Bond is not really sufficient The real answers are as follows:

1. No Mr Bond I intend TO KILL YOU. Goldfinger's cutting retort to James Bond's question

2. ShOCKING JB alias Sean Connery,also in Goldfinger, after he threw the radio set into the villain's bath

Yes both the best Bond and, in my opinion, film to although not really qualified to judge not having seen more than 3 or 4

3. You aint heard NOTHING YET. Al Jolson before The Jazz Singer.

Evidently not actually the very first Talkie.

4. I shot an arrow in the air IT FELL TO EARTH IN BERKELEY SQUARE. The wonderfully sardonic Dennis Price shooting down one of the D'Asgoine family from her balloon flight

in King Hearts and Coronets -also wonderful Ealing Black Comedy

5. Infamy Infamy, altogether now, THEY VE ALL GOT IT IN FOR ME. Julius Caesar's actual last words as revealed by Kenneth Williams in Carry on Cleo

They dont make them like that anymore

6. I could have been A CONTENDER. Yes Marlon Brando,of course, to his brother,Rod Steiger, in On The Waterfront

The most famous ? Discuss

7. Well nobody's PERFECT ! Joe E Brown when Jack Lemon disguised as a woman who Joe has been chasing, finally has to reveal he is a man

Said to be the best ever last line of a film ,and which itself just edges no.8 for my all time favourite.

8. He's not coming out. HE'S BEEN A VERY NAUGHTY BOY. shouted by Poor Terry Jones as Brian's mum in Life of Brian

9. Fasten your seatbelts ITS GOING TO BE A VERY BUMPY NIGHT. Bette Davis in All About Eve

Actually known for its sharp dialogue and not just that it was an early film of a certain blonde actress

10. You know how to WHISTLE dont you. Lauren Bacall to Humphrey Bogart in TO Have and To Have Not

Probably blowing cigarette smoke in his face as she spoke

11. Aie AIE Aie AIE Aie AIE Fay Wray when the lovesick King Kong held her on top of the Empire State Building

Made in 1933 but she is still said to be the best screamer in the business and Kong the best monster film

12. Happy BIRTHDAY Mister PRESIDENT sung by MM to John Kennedy but not quite in the manner we are used to

   And evidently it was too that night

Apologies for the Kong question which I now realise was almost impossible so anybody who got them all right except that one can still go to a cinema of choice and shout through the letterbox for the free seat.

And as compensation, to finish, here is a short and what should be a fairly easy quiz as each question has the same short one word answer.

When the PM or a Government Minister makes the following statements how many times does he not mean exactly the opposite ?

1. I want to make this absolutely clear

2. He was following the rules

3. We are all in this together

Best of Luck

Bob

30th May

Gladys

My kaftan was at the front of my wardrobe this morning. Still worn these days but it took me back to the 60's and 70's- hippies etc. So comfortable and I had a dress and a couple of tops. So today while walking I am listening to the Beach Boys. I never went to San Francisco with flowers in my hair, saw the Musical Hair, burnt my bra or smoked a joint! Is it too late? (Another get together this afternoon with the neighbours in Vale Close- ostensibly because it is Sandra and Steves 34th wedding anniversary- I would go if it was the anniversary of the first pair of wellington boots they had bought!!) Have a good weekend, be with you again on Monday
Xxxxx

Shirley

I had one just like it covers lots of cakes Chocs etcxxx

enjoy partyxx

Ian

I remember you wearing that kaftan.

Never too late to do those things.

Enjoy the party!
Xxx

<u>1st June</u>

Gladys

As we start this new month and easing of lockdown, some children back at school, shielding among us allowed out, my thoughts went to holidays and how different they are this year. So, when I opened my wardrobe , there hanging, drooping from a hanger was a memory of holidays in the 1950's- my knitted swimming costume! Now who didn't have one at that time? We would go running down through the crowded beach at Ramsgate, splashing in the water, to come out later with the costume heavy and soaking wet having stretched down as far as our knees!
Even though this costume has been hanging and stretching for many many years, it was a struggle putting it on and I am hoping that the

moth holes don't unravel too much while I am walking, or I could end up just wearing strands of wool!
Love to all of you–
Please take care
Xxxx

Janet

Love it! Made me laugh Glad. I remember having a blue one with white sailboats on it, and making friends on the beach with a little girl wearing exactly the same.
At least not so windy today, so it won't be whistling through the moth holes! Soon half the year will be gone and the longest day. Big day for many returning to school and workplaces...let's hope all stay safe. Going to be a slower pace in your flip flops today I think!xx

2nd June

Gladys

Do you remember the technicolour musical movies, Carousel, Oklahoma, Seven Brides for Seven Brothers, Annie get your Gun etc etc. with the all American girl, often Doris Day? Today I am wearing a flared gingham dress, have freckles and my hair is in pigtails, will be positively dancing around!

Ang was a star on bbc breakfast television again this morning. The reference to Glad all over - when you all buy Ian's latest book, Quarton, the Coding available on Amazon as a paperback or kindle, you will see that it is dedicated to ME! You can imagine how I felt when I opened the book yesterday to see that!

My walking will have even more of a spring in it today.

Xxx

Janet

Great! Such lovely films with feel good factor. Doubt they could make such good ones today, which is a shame. The outfit so typical for those times. Always came from the cinema feeling happy, which I think can't be said about many films today as so much violence in many of them...and tv dramas too. Can imagine the spring in your step thinking of those lovely films! Xx

3rd June

Gladys

Today I am listening to Queen dressed as Freddie Mercury in the "I want to break free" video. Black short wig, pink sleeveless top, black shiny plastic mini skirt and pushing a hoover! And of course the infamous moustache! I think we all feel we want to break free at this time! My breaking free today is meeting Ian at the garden centre and getting some plants etc. All social distancing of course and no coffee and scone in the cafe.
Take your 'lert' and break free.
Xxx

Janet

Lovely! Bet you caused a stir at the garden centre in that outfit Glad. Shame not able to have scone and cups, but moustache would have fallen in the cup! Shame not so warm and sunny today, but been nice whilst it lasted. However, if temperature drops any lower, may have to put the heating on!! Enjoy freedom but be safe still!xx

4th June

Gladys

As I start the final week of my 12week target, my wardrobe is looking very sparse, but there, in all its glory was the monkey suit that I am wearing for my walk today. I must admit I had purposely overlooked it, although it is probably more comfortable than the dalek or the space suit. Thank goodness it is a bit cooler! I don't think I shall be swinging from any trees, or carrying Fay Wray up the Empire State Building (finding climbing stairs a pain these days), but I do have a craving for bananas!

Janet

Love it! Your wardrobe must have elastic sides! Have you forgotten your Anna and the King dress, so elegant, and of course the Suddenly modern Millie outfit. If it turns wet, could always use the singing in the rain gear, and I can just see you swinging round the lamppost waving a brolly! Hope don't melt in today's outfit, despite being cooler! xx

<h1 style="text-align:center">5th June</h1>

Gladys

Like me, I know that when this lockdown started , we all made lists of projects, activities etc. to keep us occupied while staying home, staying alert and staying safe! In my case, some more successful than others(cooking- good/ slimming-bad). Want to share with you my reason for wearing todays outfit. A grass skirt, lei, flower in my hair- Hawaii. I decided it would be a good opportunity to learn a musical instrument! So borrowed Ians ukulele, bought a music book and tuner, found a very nice man on the internet who was teaching ukulele over 10 lessons. How hard could it be? Very hard! After very hurt finger tips, I have realised that my hands no longer work like they used to, co-ordination is very poor, and singing along and strumming is awful. Also basically am just no good. So have said goodbye to Andy, after just one lesson over and over again, will be handing back the ukulele, and have realised I am not going to be Essex answer to George Formby - but the grass skirt is lovely.

P.s. has anyone got a triangle I could have ? Xx

Abbey

Suggest you try pot and a spoon - alternative percussion!

6th June

Gladys

To finish the week on a cheerful note. One of the (very) many activities/ classes I have taken part in over the years was line dancing with Shirley. So today I am wearing, jeans, check shirt, neckerchief, boots and cowboy hat as I dance my way around the house.
So, thumbs in the top of the jeans, walk, forward, back, step ball change, Achy Breaky Heart and off we go!
Have good weekend- shame about the weather
Be with you Monday
Keep dancing.....xx

Ang

Thanks, Glad. I remember doing a line dancing class on one of our lovely breaks at Centerparcs. Hilarious!

8th June

Gladys

Today I am 'slobbing ' around in my PJ's while walking. My stress levels are quite high because this afternoon I have an appointment at the eye hospital for my next injection! My anxiety is not for the injection, but how is it all going to work? Ian is taking me and collecting me as I am unable to drive, I shall be masked/gloved in the back of his car with the window open. I am sure that the hospital has it all worked out but nevertheless I have decided to relax this morning and try not to get too stressed out.
By the way I have a jumper on top of my pj's cos it cold!!
'See' you tomorrow
Xxx

Bob

I'm sure it will go well. Good idea to have an open window so all those followers you have amassed can see you better when you give the Royal Wave.
Love Bob

Maureen R

*Good luck with it all. I am sure it will be fine.
Are you going in your PJ's? I would advise
against it. MX*

<u>9th June</u>

Gladys

First, thank you for all your thoughts yesterday
when I was being a complete 'wuss' about my
visit to the eye hospital, of course it was fine,
from my chauffeur to the injection.! Social
distancing masks sanitiser etc. It was eerily quiet
as only about 10 chairs in the eye waiting room
and everyone wearing masks, so little
conversation! Still took 2 1/2 hours though but
very grateful to all staff etc. Will it be the same
at my next visit in 2 months?
Back to my penultimate e mail/ costume. I can't
let these past 12 weeks go by without thinking of
France. Tom and I had so many fantastic
holidays with family and friends, often spent
weekends on a trip by coach or car or in our
motor caravan, days by boat and later
Eurotunnel (boxes of wine!!) visits to Jacqui,
and with Maureen and Trish to French circle and
French language classes in this country. My

first holiday abroad was to France age 14 to stay with a penfriend and my last trip abroad was to Paris on my birthday with Abbey. Erquy was a place that we loved and we spent many holidays there with family and friends, and as many of you know we left a little bit of Tom there on our last family holiday. So, from an almost empty wardrobe, I have my homage to all that's french, and for my walk this morning I am wearing a red frilly dress, frilly pants, fishnet stockings, and suspenders a la folies bergere! Carry that image in your head of me doing the can can while holding tightly to my walking stick!
Adieu
A la demain
Xxxx

Ian

Erquy - right up there with one of my favourite places in the world.

Mum's penultimate walk in costume. All these weeks showing what she can can do do.
Xxx

10th June

Gladys

And now the end is near
And so I face the final costume
My wardrobe is empty just as I reached my
target of 12 weeks!
Thank you all for indulging me in my fantasies, I
have had such fun writing them and it made me
do my exercise every morning, which I did
without fail- honest! Also thank you for the
many comments , they were great.
Now for some statistics:
During the 12 weeks I needed a new battery for
my car
- a new oven
- Tv repaired
- Hearing aid repaired

My clothes are tighter
My hair is longer and straggly
I have walked **4 marathons plus1.36 miles**
Total: **2612262** steps
And worn **72** different costumes!

Lovely surprise this morning, Ian came and
decorated the garden with pennants for my final
e mail walk. (good job I had decided not to wear
my birthday suit).

I shall continue to exercise, probably not at the same time each day, but now I have to go back to my empty wardrobe and investigate the door at the back- what will be there? Would be great if all of you were there.
Lots and lots of love to you all
Stay safe
Stay well
And thanks again
Gladysxxxx

Abbey

You look gorgeous granny. Well done! Xxx

Wendy

You have done so well. I will miss your daily attire. It would put me in a happier frame of mind to face the sometimes tedium of the day ahead. Like you though the exercise hasn't done much for my figure!! Also hair out of control, nails back to square one and a general lack of I don't know what. Keep in touch. Wendy XX

Janet

Love it! Well done Glad. Sad it's all over, but you could perhaps do some mix n match with the worn outfits, although with shops set to open Monday, have some retail therapy to replenish the wardrobe. Have enjoyed the posts each morning, and imagined you tramping around your estate dressed so colourfully at times. As regards to statistics and items needing To be replaced, I wondered how the flooring had fared.. ..is there sign of a well trodden path across the wood....are the chairs and table needing wedges to stop them rocking? Is a small pool forming on the deck when it rains? Does it feel like walking on the waters edge as you go down the hallway on a now sloping path? Well done for your stamina, and a shame it's not marathon weekend at Stratford, since you'd be well prepared for it! Now need to get these daily blogs printed off as a personal memory of your eightieth year!

Keep safe lots love xxx

Hoping the nightmares about me in my outfits
have stopped now.

To the Cast...

Daphne
Brian and Maureen
Bob
Janet
Maureen R.
Shirley
Edna
Wendy
Eileen
Jill and Bryan
Colin
Pat
Jo
Ian
Ang
Jacqui
Abbey

Thank you – it was a lot of fun.

Acknowledgements:

Joe for sorting out the order of my emails and putting it into a format that could be understood.

Ian for his help in publishing the book

And to Boris for giving me this wonderful opportunity

Published by Gladallover Publishers
September 2020

Printed in Great Britain
by Amazon